EASY
Cupcakes

EASY
Cupcakes

Love Food ® is an imprint of Parragon Books Ltd

Parragon
Queen Street House
4 Queen Street
Bath BA1 1HE, UK

Copyright © Parragon Books Ltd 2009

Love Food ® and the accompanying heart device is a trademark of Parragon Books Ltd

Additional photography by Clive Streeter
Additional recipes and home economy by Angela Drake
Introduction text by Susanna Tee

All rights reserved. No part of this publication may be reproduced, stored in a retrieval system, or transmitted, in any form or by any means, electronic, mechanical, photocopying, recording, or otherwise, without the prior permission of the copyright holder.

ISBN: 978-1-4075-5628-4

Printed in Indonesia

NOTES FOR THE READER
• This book uses imperial, metric, and US cup measurements. Follow the same units of measurement throughout; do not mix imperial and metric.
• All spoon measurements are level: teaspoons are assumed to be 5 ml, and tablespoons are assumed to be 15 ml.
• Unless otherwise stated, milk is assumed to be low fat and eggs are medium. The times given are an approximate guide only.
• Some recipes contain nuts. If you are allergic to nuts you should avoid using them and any products containing nuts.
• Recipes using raw or very lightly cooked eggs should be avoided by infants, the elderly, pregnant women, convalescents, and anyone suffering from illness.

Contents

Introduction

Exquisite, pretty, and unique are all words used to describe cupcakes. We all need a treat from time to time and a cupcake is the perfect answer.

There's a cupcake for every occasion and for any age, from special days, such as a child's birthday, to Christmas, a wedding, or Easter. They can be eaten as desserts, at coffee time, with afternoon tea, or as a snack time treat. They also make the perfect gift for those difficult-to-buy-for friends and are ideal for a cake sale. For children's parties, it is worth remembering that they can be popped straight into party bags.

The Cupcake's History

There are two schools of thought as to the origination of the cupcake. One thought is credited to the fact that the ingredients were originally measured by bakers in standard sized cups, instead of weights and measures, and proof of this is illustrated in some old cookery books. Another thought is credited to the cakes being baked in a tea cup and again, this is evident in old cookery books. Today, the term "cupcake" is used for a small cake baked in a fluted paper or foil baking case, a cup, or a cup-shaped mould. The cupcake is also sometimes called a fairy cake, probably because they are small, light, and delicate. Their base is made with the basic plain cake mixture with a simple iced topping or a dusting of confectioners' sugar.

The Ingredients

Cupcakes are simple and easy to make and you will probably find that you already have most of the ingredients needed to make them in your refrigerator and store cupboard. Self-rising flour, butter or margarine, superfine sugar, and eggs are all that are needed for a basic mixture. The addition of chocolate or cocoa powder is always popular and other additional ingredients include vanilla, spices, fresh and dried fruits, and nuts. As with large cakes, a topping of buttercream or a decoration is characteristic of these miniature versions, so keep a supply of toppings in the pantry, such as sprinkles, hundreds and thousands, sugar strands, silver or gold dragées, chocolate flowers, and edible sugar flower shapes.

The Basic Cupcake Recipe

If you want to make up a batch for your own creations, this is the basic mixture that will make 12 standard-size cupcakes: 4 oz/ 115 g softened butter or soft-tub margarine, 4 oz/115 g superfine sugar, 4 oz/115 g self-rising flour, and 2 eggs. For a chocolate mixture, replace 1 tablespoon of the flour with 1 tablespoon of cocoa powder. Fill the paper cases about two-thirds full and bake in the oven at 350°F/180°C for about 20 minutes. To make sufficient buttercream icing to top them, you will need 3oz/85g butter and 6 oz/175 g confectioners' sugar. For a glaze icing you will need 6 oz/175 g confectioners' sugar and 2–3 teaspoons water.

Baking Cupcakes

Cupcakes are best when freshly baked and baked in a fluted paper or foil baking case. The cases not only retain the cake's shape and make them an ideal individual serving, but also help to keep them moist and fresh for longer. They are available in mini, standard, and large (muffin) sizes in a variety of colors and decorations. Reusable, silicone baking cases in bright colors are also available.

Perfect Results

Baking cupcakes is a science as well as an art, so unless you are very experienced in baking generally, it is important to follow the recipes exactly. Read through the recipe and collect all the ingredients and equipment together before you start—this will make the process of baking the cupcakes a lot easier. Do not be tempted to cut corners. It is worth noting that there may be some variables that may affect the end result and the biggest of these is usually the oven. Because temperatures can vary from appliance to appliance, to ensure the best results use the baking times specified in the recipes as a guide only.

Do not be tempted to check the oven too early, which could adversely affect the cupcakes, but do check just a few minutes before the end of the baking time to see how the cupcakes are progressing.

Equipment

Measuring scales, mixing bowls, a wooden spoon, baking trays, and bun trays are all the items you'll need to begin making cupcakes. But as soon as the baking bug bites, you can gradually add other tools to those basics, such as an electric handheld mixer, which will certainly make the job easier and quicker.

1

Fun & Fancy

Pink & White Cupcakes

makes 16

generous ¾ cup self-rising flour

1 tsp baking powder

½ cup butter, softened

generous ½ cup superfine sugar

2 eggs, lightly beaten

1 tbsp milk

few drops red food coloring

for the topping

1 egg white

generous ¾ cup superfine sugar

2 tbsp hot water

large pinch of cream of tartar

2 tbsp raspberry jam

3 tbsp dry unsweetened coconut, lightly toasted

Preheat the oven to 350°F/180°C. Put 16 paper cases in 2 muffin pans or put 16 double-layer paper cases on a large baking sheet.

Sift the flour and baking powder into a bowl. Add the butter, sugar, and eggs and, using an electric handheld mixer, beat together until smooth. Mix together the milk and food coloring and mix into the mixture until evenly blended. Spoon the mixture into the paper cases.

Bake the cupcakes in the preheated oven for 20 minutes, or until risen and golden brown. Transfer to a wire rack and let cool.

To make the topping, put the egg white, sugar, water, and cream of tartar in a heatproof bowl set over a saucepan of simmering water. Using an electric handheld mixer, beat for 5–6 minutes, until the mixture is thick and makes soft peaks when the mixer is lifted out.

Spread a layer of raspberry jam over each cupcake, and then swirl over the frosting. Sprinkle with the toasted coconut.

Rose Petal Cupcakes

makes 12

8 tbsp butter, softened

generous ½ cup superfine sugar

2 eggs, lightly beaten

1 tbsp milk

few drops of extract of rose oil

¼ tsp vanilla extract

scant 1¼ cups self-rising flour

crystallized rose petals and silver dragées (cake decoration balls), to decorate

for the frosting

6 tbsp butter, softened

1½ cups confectioners' sugar

pink or purple food coloring (optional)

Preheat the oven to 400°F/200°C. Put 12 paper cases in a muffin pan, or put 12 double-layer paper cases on a baking sheet.

Put the butter and sugar in a bowl and beat together until light and fluffy. Gradually add the eggs, beating well after each addition. Stir in the milk, rose oil extract, and vanilla extract then, using a metal spoon, fold in the flour. Spoon the batter into the paper cases. Bake the cupcakes in the preheated oven for 12–15 minutes until well risen and golden brown. Transfer to a wire rack and let cool.

To make the frosting, put the butter in a large bowl and beat until fluffy. Sift in the confectioners' sugar and mix well together. If wished, add a few drops of pink or purple food coloring to complement the rose petals.

When the cupcakes are cold, spread the frosting on top of each cake. Top with 1–2 candied rose petals and sprinkle with silver dragées to decorate.

Poppy Seed & Orange Cupcakes

makes 12

2 tbsp poppy seeds

2 tbsp hot milk

6 tbsp butter, softened

scant ½ cup superfine sugar

finely grated rind of ½ orange

1 large egg, lightly beaten

¾ cup self-rising flour

for the frosting

6 tbsp butter, softened

finely grated rind of ½ orange

1½ cups confectioners' sugar

1–2 tbsp orange juice

Preheat the oven to 350°F/180°C. Put 12 paper cases in a muffin pan or put 12 double-layer paper cases on a baking sheet. Place the poppy seeds and milk in a small bowl and set aside for 10 minutes.

Put the butter, sugar, and orange rind in a bowl and beat together until light and fluffy. Gradually beat in the egg. Sift in the flour and, using a metal spoon, fold gently into the mixture with the poppy seeds and milk. Spoon the mixture into the paper cases.

Bake the cupcakes in the preheated oven for 20 minutes, or until risen and golden brown. Transfer to a wire rack and let cool.

To make the frosting, put the butter and orange rind in a bowl and beat until fluffy. Gradually beat in the confectioners' sugar and enough orange juice to make a smooth and creamy frosting. Swirl the frosting over the top of the cupcakes.

Fairy Cupcakes

makes 16

1/2 cup butter

heaping 1/2 cup superfine sugar

2 eggs, beaten

1 cup self-rising flour

sugar flowers, sprinkles, candied cherries, and/ or chocolate strands, to decorate

for the frosting

1¾ cups confectioners' sugar

about 2 tbsp warm water

a few drops of food coloring (optional)

Preheat the oven to 375°F/190°C. Place 16 paper cases into 2 shallow muffin pans.

Place the butter and sugar in a large bowl and cream together with a wooden spoon or electric handheld mixer until pale and fluffy.

Gradually add the eggs, beating well after each addition. Fold in the flour lightly and evenly using a metal spoon. Divide the mixture among the paper liners and bake in the preheated oven for 15–20 minutes. Cool on a wire rack.

For the frosting, sift the confectioners' sugar into a bowl and stir in just enough water to mix to a smooth paste that is thick enough to coat the back of a wooden spoon. Stir in a few drops of food coloring, if using, then spread the frosting over the cupcakes and decorate as desired.

Caramel Cupcakes

makes 12

6 tbsp butter, softened

¼ cup dark brown sugar

1 tbsp dark corn syrup

1 large egg, lightly beaten

¾ cup self-rising flour

1 tsp grated nutmeg

2 tbsp milk

for the frosting

½ cup light brown sugar

1 small egg white

1 tbsp hot water

pinch of cream of tartar

Preheat the oven to 350°F/180°C. Put 12 paper cases in a muffin pan or put 12 double-layer paper cases on a baking sheet.

Put the butter, sugar, and corn syrup in a bowl and beat together until light and fluffy. Gradually beat in the egg. Sift in the flour and, using a metal spoon, fold gently into the mixture with the nutmeg and milk. Spoon the mixture into the paper cases.

Bake the cupcakes in the preheated oven for 15–20 minutes, or until risen and golden brown. Transfer to a wire rack and let cool.

To make the frosting, put all the ingredients in a heatproof bowl set over a saucepan of simmering water. Using an electric handheld mixer, beat for 5–6 minutes, until the mixture is thick and softly peaking when the mixer is lifted. Swirl the frosting over the cupcakes.

Drizzled Honey Cupcakes

makes 12

scant ⅝ cup self-rising flour

¼ tsp ground cinnamon

pinch of ground cloves

pinch of grated nutmeg

6 tbsp butter, softened

generous ⅜ cup superfine sugar

1 tbsp honey

finely grated rind of 1 orange

2 eggs, lightly beaten

¾ cup walnut pieces, chopped

for the topping

⅛ cup walnut pieces, chopped

¼ tsp ground cinnamon

2 tbsp honey

juice of 1 orange

Preheat the oven to 375°F/190°C. Put 12 paper cases in a muffin pan, or put 12 double-layer paper cases on a baking sheet.

Sift the flour, cinnamon, cloves, and nutmeg together into a bowl. Put the butter and sugar in a separate bowl and beat together until light and fluffy. Beat in the honey and orange rind, then gradually add the eggs, beating well after each addition. Using a metal spoon, fold in the flour mixture. Stir in the walnuts, then spoon the batter into the paper cases.

Bake the cupcakes in the preheated oven for 20 minutes, or until well risen and golden brown. Transfer to a wire rack and let cool.

To make the topping, mix together the walnuts and cinnamon. Put the honey and orange juice in a pan and heat gently, stirring, until combined.

When the cupcakes have almost cooled, prick the tops all over with a fork or skewer and then drizzle with the warm honey mixture. Sprinkle the walnut mixture over the top of each cupcake and serve warm or cold.

Mini Candy Cupcakes

makes 18

generous ⅓ cup self-rising flour

¼ tsp baking powder

4 tbsp soft margarine

¼ cup superfine sugar

1 egg, lightly beaten

candies, such as gum drops, licorice, and sugar-coated chocolate candies, to decorate

for the frosting

¾ cup confectioners' sugar

2–3 tsp water

few drops pink food coloring (optional)

Preheat the oven to 350°F/180°C. Put 18 paper mini muffin cases on a baking sheet.

Sift the flour and baking powder into a bowl. Add the margarine, sugar, and egg and, using an electric handheld mixer, beat together until smooth. Spoon the mixture into the paper cases.

Bake the cupcakes in the preheated oven for 15–20 minutes, until risen and golden brown. Transfer to a wire rack and let cool.

To make the frosting, sift the confectioners' sugar into a bowl and beat in the water to make a smooth thick frosting. Stir in the pink food coloring, if using. Spoon a little frosting in the center of each cupcake and decorate each with a candy. Let set.

Frosted Peanut Butter Cupcakes

makes 16

4 tbsp butter, softened

generous 1⅛ cups firmly packed brown sugar

generous ⅓ cup crunchy peanut butter

2 eggs, lightly beaten

1 tsp vanilla extract

scant 1⅝ cups all-purpose flour

2 tsp baking powder

generous ⅓ cup milk

for the frosting

scant 1 cup full-fat soft cream cheese

2 tbsp butter, softened

2 cups confectioners' sugar

Preheat the oven to 350°F/180°C. Put 16 paper cases into 2 shallow muffin pans or put 16 double-layer paper cases on a large baking sheet.

Put the butter, sugar, and peanut butter in a bowl and beat together for 1–2 minutes, or until well mixed. Gradually add the eggs, beating well after each addition, then add the vanilla extract. Sift in the flour and baking powder and then, using a metal spoon, fold them into the mixture, alternating with the milk. Spoon the batter into the paper cases.

Bake the cupcakes in the preheated oven for 25 minutes, or until well risen and golden brown. Transfer to a wire rack and let cool.

To make the frosting, put the cream cheese and butter in a large bowl and, using an electric handheld mixer, beat together until smooth. Sift the confectioners' sugar into the mixture, then beat together until well mixed.

When the cupcakes are cold, spread the frosting on top of each cupcake, swirling it with a round-bladed knife. Store the cupcakes in the refrigerator until ready to serve.

Chewy Oatmeal Cupcakes

makes 8

3 tbsp soft margarine

3 tbsp raw brown sugar

1 tbsp dark corn syrup

$\frac{2}{3}$ cup rolled oats

4 tbsp butter, softened

$\frac{1}{4}$ cup superfine sugar

1 large egg, lightly beaten

generous $\frac{1}{3}$ cup self-rising flour

Preheat the oven to 375°F/190°C. Put 8 paper cases in a muffin pan or put 8 double-layer paper cases on a baking sheet.

Place the margarine, raw brown sugar, and corn syrup in a small saucepan and heat gently until the margarine has melted. Stir in the oats. Set aside.

Put the butter and superfine sugar in a bowl and beat together until light and fluffy. Gradually beat in the egg. Sift in the flour and, using a metal spoon, fold gently into the mixture. Spoon the mixture into the paper cases. Gently spoon the oatmeal mixture over the top.

Bake the cupcakes in the preheated oven for 20 minutes, or until golden brown. Transfer to a wire rack and let cool.

Queen Cupcakes

makes 18

8 tbsp butter, softened

generous ½ cup superfine sugar

2 large eggs, lightly beaten

4 tsp lemon juice

scant 1¼ cups self-rising flour

¾ cup currants

2–4 tbsp milk, if necessary

Preheat the oven to 375°F/190°C. Put 18 paper cases in 2 muffin pans or put 18 double-layer paper cases on 2 baking sheets.

Put the butter and sugar in a bowl and beat together until light and fluffy. Gradually beat in the eggs, then beat in the lemon juice with 1 tablespoon of the flour. Using a metal spoon, fold in the remaining flour and the currants, adding a little milk if necessary to give a soft dropping consistency. Spoon the batter into the paper cases.

Bake the cupcakes in the preheated oven for 15–20 minutes, or until well risen and golden brown. Transfer to a wire rack and let cool.

Fudge & Raisin Cupcakes

makes 10

4 oz/115 g vanilla fudge, cut into small chunks

1 tbsp milk

6 tbsp butter, softened

3 tbsp light brown sugar

1 large egg, lightly beaten

¾ cup self-rising flour

3 tbsp raisins

Preheat the oven to 375°F/190°C. Put 10 paper cases in a muffin pan or put 10 double-layer paper cases on a baking sheet.

Put half the fudge in a heatproof bowl with the milk and set over a saucepan of gently simmering water until the fudge has melted. Remove from the heat and stir until smooth. Cool for 10 minutes.

Put the butter and sugar into a bowl and beat together until light and fluffy. Gradually beat in the egg. Sift in the flour and, using a metal spoon, fold gently into the mixture with the raisins. Fold in the melted fudge. Spoon the mixture into the paper cases. Scatter the remaining fudge chunks over the cupcakes.

Bake the cupcakes in the preheated oven for 15–20 minutes, or until risen and golden brown. Transfer to a wire rack and let cool.

Sticky Gingerbread Cupcakes

makes 16

generous ¾ cup all-purpose flour

2 tsp ground ginger

¾ tsp ground cinnamon

1 piece of preserved ginger, chopped

¾ tsp baking soda

4 tbsp milk

6 tbsp butter, softened

generous ⅓ cup firmly packed brown sugar

2 tbsp molasses

2 eggs, lightly beaten

pieces of preserved ginger, to decorate

for the frosting

6 tbsp butter, softened

1½ cups confectioners' sugar

2 tbsp ginger syrup from the preserved ginger jar

Preheat the oven to 325°F/160°C. Put 16 paper cases in 2 muffin pans or put 16 double-layer paper cases on 2 baking sheets.

Sift the flour, ground ginger, and cinnamon together into a bowl. Add the chopped ginger and toss in the flour mixture until well coated. In a separate bowl, dissolve the baking soda in the milk.

Put the butter and sugar in a bowl and beat together until fluffy. Beat in the molasses, then gradually add the eggs, beating well after each addition. Beat in the flour mixture, then gradually beat in the milk. Spoon the batter into the paper cases.

Bake the cupcakes in the preheated oven for 20 minutes, or until well risen and golden brown. Transfer to a wire rack and let cool.

To make the frosting, put the butter in a bowl and beat until fluffy. Sift in the confectioners' sugar, add the ginger syrup, and beat together until smooth and creamy. Slice the preserved ginger into thin slivers or chop finely.

When the cupcakes are cold, spread the frosting on top of each cupcake, then decorate with pieces of ginger.

Frosted Lemon-Almond Cupcakes

makes 16

½ cup butter, softened

generous ½ cup superfine sugar

finely grated rind of ½ lemon

2 large eggs, lightly beaten

1¼ cups self-rising flour

generous ⅓ cup ground almonds

⅓ cup candied citron peel, thinly sliced

for the frosting

½ cup confectioners' sugar

3 tsp warm water

Preheat the oven to 350°F/180°C. Put 16 paper cases in 2 muffin pans or put 16 double-layer paper cases on a baking sheet.

Put the butter, sugar, and lemon rind in a bowl and beat together until light and fluffy. Gradually beat in the eggs. Sift in the flour and, using a metal spoon, fold gently into the mixture with the ground almonds. Spoon the mixture into the paper cases. Put a slice of citron peel on the top of each cupcake.

Bake the cupcakes in the preheated oven for 20–25 minutes, or until risen and golden brown. Transfer to a wire rack and let cool.

To make the frosting, sift the confectioners' sugar into a bowl and add enough of the warm water to make a runny frosting. Using a pastry brush, glaze the top of each cupcake with the frosting. Let set.

Rocky Road Cupcakes

makes 12

2 tbsp cocoa powder

2 tbsp hot water

½ cup butter, softened

½ cup superfine sugar

2 eggs, lightly beaten

generous ¾ cup self-rising flour

for the topping

¼ cup chopped mixed nuts

3½ oz/100 g milk chocolate, melted

4 oz/115 g mini marshmallows

¼ cup candied cherries, chopped

Preheat the oven to 350°F/180°C. Put 12 paper cases in a muffin pan or put 12 double-layer paper cases on a baking sheet.

Blend the cocoa powder and hot water together and set aside. Put the butter and sugar in a bowl and beat together until light and fluffy. Gradually beat in the eggs, then beat in the blended cocoa. Sift in the flour and, using a metal spoon, fold gently into the mixture. Spoon the mixture into the paper cases.

Bake the cupcakes in the preheated oven for 20 minutes, or until risen and firm to the touch. Transfer to a wire rack and let cool.

To make the topping, stir the nuts into the melted chocolate and spread a little of the mixture over the top of the cakes. Lightly stir the marshmallows and cherries into the remaining chocolate mixture and pile on top of the cupcakes. Let set.

Sugar & Spice Cupcakes

makes 14

½ cup butter, softened

½ cup superfine sugar

2 eggs, lightly beaten

generous ¾ cup self-rising flour

2 tsp ground allspice

¼ cup mixed peel

⅓ cup candied cherries, chopped

1 tbsp milk

4 white sugar cubes, roughly crushed

for the glaze

2 tbsp granulated sugar

3 tbsp water

Preheat the oven to 375°F/190°C. Put 14 paper cases in 2 muffin pans or put 14 double-layer paper cases on a baking sheet.

Put the butter and sugar in a bowl and beat together until light and fluffy. Gradually beat in the eggs. Sift in the flour and half the allspice and, using a metal spoon, fold gently into the mixture with the mixed peel, cherries, and milk. Spoon the mixture into the paper cases.

Mix together the crushed sugar cubes and remaining allspice and sprinkle over the top of the cupcakes.

Bake the cupcakes in the preheated oven for 15–20 minutes, or until risen and firm to touch. Transfer to a wire rack.

To make the glaze, place the sugar and water in a small pan and heat until the sugar dissolves. Bring to a boil and boil, without stirring, for 2–3 minutes, until reduced and syrupy. Brush the hot syrup over the warm cupcakes. Let cool.

Lemon Cornmeal Cupcakes

makes 14

½ cup butter, softened

½ cup superfine sugar

finely grated rind and juice of ½ lemon

2 eggs lightly beaten

generous ⅓ cup all-purpose flour

1 tsp baking powder

⅓ cup quick-cooking cornmeal

crystallized violets, to decorate

for the frosting

5½ oz/150 g mascarpone cheese

2 tsp finely grated lemon rind

¼ cup confectioners' sugar

Preheat the oven to 350°F/180°C. Put 14 paper cases in 2 muffin pans or put 14 double-layer paper cases on a baking sheet.

Put the butter and sugar in a bowl and beat together until light and fluffy. Beat in the lemon rind and juice. Gradually beat in the eggs. Sift in the flour and baking powder and, using a metal spoon, fold gently into the mixture with the cornmeal. Spoon the mixture into the paper cases.

Bake the cupcakes in the preheated oven for 20 minutes, or golden brown and firm to the touch. Transfer to a wire rack and let cool.

To make the frosting, beat the mascarpone cheese until smooth, then beat in the lemon rind and confectioners' sugar. Spread the frosting over the cupcakes. Store the cupcakes in the refrigerator until ready to serve. Decorate each cupcake with a crystallized violet just before serving.

2

Chocolate Heaven

Tiny Chocolate Cupcakes with Ganache Frosting

makes 20

4 tbsp unsalted butter, softened

¼ cup superfine sugar

1 large egg, lightly beaten

scant ½ cup self-rising flour

2 tbsp unsweetened cocoa

1 tbsp milk

20 chocolate-coated coffee beans, to decorate (optional)

for the frosting

3½ oz/100 g semisweet chocolate

⅓ cup heavy cream

Preheat the oven to 375°F/190°C. Put 20 double-layer mini paper cases on 2 baking sheets.

Put the butter and sugar in a bowl and beat together until light and fluffy. Gradually beat in the egg. Sift in the flour and cocoa and then, using a metal spoon, fold them into the mixture. Stir in the milk.

Take a pastry bag fitted with a large plain tip, fill it with the batter, and pipe it into the paper cases, filling each one until half full.

Bake the cakes in the preheated oven for 10–15 minutes, or until well risen and firm to the touch. Transfer to a wire rack to cool.

To make the frosting, break the chocolate into a pan and add the cream. Heat gently, stirring all the time, until the chocolate has melted. Pour into a large heatproof bowl and, using a handheld electric mixer, beat the mixture for 10 minutes, or until thick, glossy, and cool.

Take a pastry bag fitted with a large star tip, fill it with the frosting, and pipe a swirl on top of each cupcake. Alternatively, spoon the frosting over the top of each cupcake. Chill in the refrigerator for 1 hour before serving. Serve decorated with a chocolate-coated coffee bean (if using).

Double Chocolate Cupcakes

makes 18

3 oz/85 g white chocolate

1 tbsp milk

generous ¾ cup self-rising flour

½ tsp baking powder

½ cup butter, softened

generous ½ cup superfine sugar

2 eggs

1 tsp vanilla extract

for the topping

5 oz/140 g milk chocolate

18 white chocolate buttons

Preheat the oven to 375°F/190°C. Put 18 paper cases in 2 muffin pans or put 18 double-layer paper cases on a large baking sheet.

Break the white chocolate into a heatproof bowl and add the milk. Set the bowl over a saucepan of simmering water and heat until melted. Remove from the heat and stir gently until smooth.

Sift the flour and baking powder into a bowl. Add the butter, sugar, eggs, and vanilla extract and, using an electric handheld mixer, beat together until smooth. Fold in the melted white chocolate. Spoon the mixture into the paper cases.

Bake in the preheated oven for 20 minutes, or until risen and golden brown. Transfer to a wire rack and let cool.

To make the topping, break the chocolate into a heatproof bowl and set the bowl over a saucepan of gently simmering water until melted. Cool for 5 minutes, then spread over the top of the cupcakes. Decorate each cupcake with a chocolate button.

Mocha Cupcakes with Whipped Cream

makes 20

2 tbsp instant espresso
coffee powder

6 tbsp unsalted butter

6 tbsp superfine sugar

1 tbsp honey

scant 1 cup water

1½ cups all-purpose flour

2 tbsp unsweetened cocoa

1 tsp baking soda

3 tbsp milk

1 large egg, lightly beaten

for the topping

1 cup whipping cream

unsweetened cocoa, sifted,
for dusting

Preheat the oven to 350°F/180°C. Put 20 paper cases in 2 muffin pans or put 20 double-layer paper cases on 2 baking sheets.

Put the coffee powder, butter, sugar, honey, and water in a saucepan and heat gently, stirring, until the sugar has dissolved. Bring to a boil, then reduce the heat and let simmer for 5 minutes. Pour into a large heatproof bowl and let cool.

When the mixture has cooled, sift in the flour and cocoa. Dissolve the baking soda in the milk, then add to the mixture with the egg and beat together until smooth. Spoon the batter into the paper cases.

Bake the cupcakes in the preheated oven for 15–20 minutes, or until well risen and firm to the touch. Transfer to a wire rack to cool.

For the topping, whip the cream in a bowl until it holds its shape. Just before serving, spoon heaping teaspoonfuls of cream on top of each cake, then dust lightly with sifted cocoa. Store the cupcakes in the refrigerator until ready to serve.

Chocolate Hazelnut Cupcakes

makes 18

¾ cup butter, softened

generous ½ cup light brown sugar

2 large eggs, lightly beaten

2 tbsp chocolate-and-hazelnut spread

1¼ cups self-rising flour

scant ½ cup blanched hazelnuts, coarsely ground

for the topping

5 tbsp chocolate-and-hazelnut spread

18 whole blanched hazelnuts

Preheat the oven to 350°F/180°C. Put 18 paper cases in 2 muffin pans or put 18 double-layer paper cases on a large baking sheet.

Put the butter and sugar in a mixing bowl and beat together until light and fluffy. Gradually beat in the eggs, then stir in the chocolate-and-hazelnut spread. Sift in the flour and, using a metal spoon, fold into the mixture with the ground hazelnuts. Spoon the mixture into the paper cases.

Bake the cupcakes in the preheated oven for 20–25 minutes, or until risen and firm to the touch. Transfer to a wire rack and let cool.

When the cupcakes are cold, swirl some chocolate-and-hazelnut spread over the top of each cupcake and top with a hazelnut.

Devil's Food Cakes with Chocolate Frosting

makes 18

3½ tbsp soft margarine

½ cup firmly packed brown sugar

2 large eggs

¾ cup all-purpose flour

½ tsp baking soda

¼ cup unsweetened cocoa

½ cup sour cream

for the frosting

4½ oz/125 g semisweet chocolate

2 tbsp superfine sugar

⅔ cup sour cream

chocolate caraque, to decorate

Preheat the oven to 350°F/180°C. Put 18 paper cases in 2 muffin pans or put 18 double-layer paper cases on 2 baking sheets.

Put the margarine, sugar, eggs, flour, baking soda, and cocoa in a large bowl and, using a handheld electric mixer, beat together until just smooth. Using a metal spoon, fold in the sour cream. Spoon the batter into the paper cases.

Bake the cupcakes in the preheated oven for 20 minutes, or until well risen and firm to the touch. Transfer to a wire rack to cool.

To make the frosting, break the chocolate into a heatproof bowl. Set the bowl over a saucepan of gently simmering water and heat until melted, stirring occasionally. Remove from the heat and let cool slightly, then whisk in the sugar and sour cream until combined. Spread the frosting over the tops of the cupcakes and let set in the refrigerator before serving. Serve decorated with chocolate caraque.

Dark & White Fudge Cupcakes

makes 20

scant 1 cup water

6 tbsp butter

generous ⅜ cup superfine sugar

1 tbsp corn syrup

3 tbsp milk

1 tsp vanilla extract

1 tsp baking soda

scant 1⅝ cups all-purpose flour

2 tbsp unsweetened cocoa

for the topping

1¾ oz/50 g semisweet chocolate

4 tbsp water

3½ tbsp butter

1¾ oz/50 g white chocolate

3 cups confectioners' sugar

for the chocolate curls

3½ oz/100 g semisweet chocolate

3½ oz/100 g white chocolate

Preheat the oven to 350°F/180°C. Put 20 paper cases in 2 muffin pans or put 20 double-layer paper cases on 2 baking sheets.

Put the water, butter, superfine sugar, and syrup in a pan. Heat gently, stirring, until the sugar has dissolved, then bring to a boil. Reduce the heat and cook gently for 5 minutes. Remove from the heat and let cool.

Meanwhile, put the milk and vanilla extract in a bowl. Add the baking soda and stir to dissolve. Sift the flour and cocoa into a separate bowl and add the syrup mixture. Stir in the milk and beat until smooth. Spoon the batter into the paper cases until they are two-thirds full.

Bake the cupcakes in the preheated oven for 20 minutes, or until well risen and firm to the touch. Transfer to a wire rack and let cool.

To make the topping, break the semisweet chocolate into a small heatproof bowl, add half the water and half the butter, and set the bowl over a pan of gently simmering water until melted. Stir until smooth and let stand over the water. Using another bowl, repeat with the white chocolate and remaining water and butter. Sift half the sugar into each bowl and beat until smooth and thick. Top the cupcakes up with the frostings. Let set. Serve decorated with chocolate curls made by shaving the chocolate with a potato peeler.

Chocolate & Orange Cupcakes

makes 16

½ cup butter, softened

generous ½ cup superfine sugar

finely grated rind and juice of ½ orange

2 eggs, lightly beaten

generous ¾ cup self-rising flour

1 oz/25 g dark chocolate, grated

for the frosting

4 oz /115 g dark chocolate, broken into pieces

2 tbsp unsalted butter

1 tbsp dark corn syrup

thin strips candied orange peel, to decorate

Preheat the oven to 350°F/180°C. Put 16 paper liner cases in 2 muffin pans or put 16 double-layer paper cases on a baking sheet.

Put the butter, sugar, and orange rind in a bowl and beat together until light and fluffy. Gradually beat in the eggs. Sift in the flour and, using a metal spoon, fold gently into the mixture with the orange juice and grated chocolate. Spoon the mixture into the paper cases.

Bake the cupcakes in the preheated oven for 20 minutes, or until risen and golden brown. Transfer to a wire rack and let cool.

To make the frosting, break the chocolate into a heatproof bowl and add the butter and syrup. Set the bowl over a saucepan of simmering water and heat until melted. Remove from the heat and stir until smooth. Cool until the frosting is thick enough to spread. Spread over the cupcakes and decorate each cupcake with a few strips of candied orange peel. Let set.

Marbled Chocolate Cupcakes

makes 21

¾ cup soft margarine

generous ¾ cup superfine sugar

3 eggs

scant 1¼ cups self-rising flour

2 tbsp milk

2 oz/55 g semisweet chocolate, melted

Preheat the oven to 350°F/180°C. Put 21 paper cases in 2 muffin pans or put 21 double-layer paper cases on a large baking tray.

Put the margarine, sugar, eggs, flour, and milk in a large bowl and, using an electric handheld mixer, beat together until just smooth.

Divide the batter between 2 bowls. Add the melted chocolate to one bowl and stir until well mixed. Using a teaspoon, and alternating the chocolate batter with the plain batter, put four half-teaspoons into each paper case.

Bake the cupcakes in the preheated oven for 20 minutes, or until well risen and springy to the touch. Transfer to a wire rack and let cool.

Pear & Chocolate Cupcakes

makes 12

½ cup margarine

generous ½ cup light brown sugar

2 eggs

¾ cup self-rising flour

½ tsp baking powder

2 tbsp cocoa powder

4 canned pear halves, drained and sliced

2 tbsp honey, warmed

Preheat the oven to 375°F/190°C. Put 12 paper cases in a muffin pan or put 12 double-layer paper cases on a baking sheet.

Put the margarine, sugar, eggs, flour, baking powder, and cocoa in a large bowl and, using an electric handheld mixer, beat together until just smooth. Spoon the mixture into the paper cases and smooth the tops. Arrange 2 pear slices on top of each cupcake.

Bake the cupcakes in the preheated oven for 20 minutes, or until risen and just firm to the touch. Transfer to a wire cooling rack. While the cupcakes are still warm, glaze with the honey. Let cool completely.

Chocolate Butterfly Cupcakes

makes 12

½ cup soft margarine

½ cup superfine sugar

1½ cups self-rising flour

2 large eggs

2 tbsp unsweetened cocoa

1 oz/25 g semisweet
chocolate, melted

confectioners' sugar,
for dusting

for the filling

6 tbsp unsalted butter,
softened

1½ cups confectioners'
sugar

1 oz/25 g semisweet
chocolate, melted

Preheat the oven to 350°F/180°C. Put 12 paper cases in a muffin pan or put 12 double-layer paper cases on a baking sheet.

Put the margarine, sugar, flour, eggs, and cocoa in a large bowl and, using a handheld electric mixer, beat together until just smooth. Beat in the melted chocolate. Spoon the batter into the paper cases, filling them three-quarters full.

Bake the cupcakes in the preheated oven for 15 minutes, or until springy to the touch. Transfer to a wire rack and let cool.

To make the filling, put the butter in a bowl and beat until fluffy. Sift in the confectioners' sugar and beat together until smooth. Add the melted chocolate and beat together until well mixed.

When the cupcakes are cooled, use a serrated knife to cut a circle from the top of each cake and then cut each circle in half. Spread or pipe a little of the buttercream into the center of each cupcake and press the 2 semicircular halves into it at an angle to resemble butterfly wings. Dust with sifted confectioners' sugar before serving.

Chocolate Cupcakes with Cream Cheese Frosting

makes 18

6 tbsp unsalted butter, softened

½ cup superfine sugar

2 eggs, lightly beaten

2 tbsp milk

⅓ cup semisweet chocolate chips

1½ cups self-rising flour

¼ cup unsweetened cocoa

for the frosting

8 oz/225 g white chocolate

⅔ cup lowfat cream cheese

chocolate curls, to decorate

Preheat the oven to 400°F/200°C. Put 18 paper cases in 2 muffin pans or put 18 double-layer paper cases on 2 baking sheets.

Put the butter and sugar in a bowl and beat together until light and fluffy. Gradually add the eggs, beating well after each addition. Add the milk, then fold in the chocolate chips. Sift the flour and cocoa, then fold into the mixture. Spoon the batter into the paper cases and smooth the tops.

Bake the cupcakes in the preheated oven for 20 minutes, or until well risen and springy to the touch. Transfer to a wire rack and let cool.

To make the frosting, break the chocolate into a small heatproof bowl and set the bowl over a saucepan of gently simmering water until melted. Let cool slightly. Put the cream cheese in a bowl and beat until softened, then beat in the slightly cooled chocolate.

Spread a little of the frosting over the top of each cupcake, then let chill in the refrigerator for 1 hour before serving. Serve decorated with the chocolate curls.

Chocolate Chip Cupcakes

makes 8

scant ½ cup soft margarine

½ cup superfine sugar

2 large eggs

scant ¾ cup self-rising flour

½ cup semisweet chocolate chips

Preheat the oven to 375°F/190°C. Put 8 muffin paper cases in a muffin pan or put 8 double-layer paper cases on a baking sheet.

Put the margarine, sugar, eggs, and flour in a large bowl and, using a handheld electric mixer, beat together until just smooth. Fold in the chocolate chips and spoon the batter into the paper cases.

Bake the cupcakes in the preheated oven for 20–25 minutes, or until well risen and golden brown. Transfer to a wire rack to cool.

Chocolate Florentine Cupcakes

makes 12

2 oz/55 g dark chocolate

6 tbsp butter

1 tbsp dark corn syrup

¼ cup soft brown sugar

generous ¾ cup self-rising flour

1 large egg, beaten

for the topping

¼ cup candied cherries, chopped

¼ cup slivered almonds

1 tbsp raisins

1 tbsp dark corn syrup

Preheat the oven to 375°F/190°C. Put 12 paper cases in a muffin pan or put 12 double-layer paper cases on a baking sheet.

Put the chocolate, butter, corn syrup, and sugar in a saucepan and heat gently, stirring occasionally, until just melted. Cool for 2 minutes. Sift the flour into a bowl.

Pour the chocolate mixture into the bowl. Add the egg and beat until thoroughly blended. Spoon the mixture into the paper cases.

Mix together the topping ingredients and gently spoon a little of the mixture on top of each cupcake.

Bake the cupcakes in the preheated oven for 15–20 minutes, or until risen and firm to the touch. Transfer to a wire rack and let cool.

Warm Molten-Centered Chocolate Cupcakes

makes 8

4 tbsp soft margarine

½ cup superfine sugar

1 large egg

½ cup self-rising flour

1 tbsp unsweetened cocoa

2 oz/55 g semisweet chocolate

confectioners' sugar, for dusting

Preheat the oven to 375°F/190°C. Put 8 paper cases in a muffin pan or put 8 double-layer paper cases on a baking sheet.

Put the margarine, sugar, egg, flour, and cocoa in a large bowl and, using a handheld electric mixer, beat together until just smooth.

Spoon half of the batter into the paper cases. Using a teaspoon, make an indentation in the center of each cake. Break the chocolate evenly into 8 squares and place a piece in each indentation, then spoon the remaining cake batter on top.

Bake the cupcakes in the preheated oven for 20 minutes, or until well risen and springy to the touch. Leave the cupcakes for 2–3 minutes before serving warm, dusted with sifted confectioners' sugar.

Wholewheat Apricot Cupcakes

makes 14

½ cup butter, softened

scant ½ cup soft brown sugar

2 tbsp honey

2 eggs, lightly beaten

generous ⅔ cup wholewheat all-purpose flour

1½ tsp baking powder

1 tsp ground allspice

½ plumped dried apricots, chopped

2 tbsp apricot jam, warmed and strained

slices of plumped dried apricots, to decorate

Preheat the oven to 375°F/190°C. Put 14 paper cases in 2 muffin pans or put 14 double-layer paper cases on a baking sheet.

Put the butter, sugar, and honey in a bowl and beat together until light and fluffy. Gradually add the eggs, beating well after each addition. Sift in the flour, baking powder, and allspice (tipping any bran left in the sifter into the bowl) and, using a metal spoon, fold them into the mixture with the chopped apricots. Spoon the mixture into the paper cases.

Bake the cupcakes in the preheated oven for 15–20 minutes, or until risen, golden brown, and firm to the touch. Transfer to a wire rack to cool.

When the cupcakes are cold, brush the apricot jam over the top of each cupcake and decorate each with a slice of apricot.

Tropical Pineapple Cupcakes with Citrus Cream Frosting

makes 12

2 slices of canned pineapple in natural juice

6 tbsp butter, softened

generous ⅜ cup superfine sugar

1 large egg, lightly beaten

scant ⅝ cup self-rising flour

1 tbsp juice from the canned pineapple

for the frosting

2 tbsp butter, softened

generous ⅜ cup soft cream cheese

grated rind of 1 lemon or lime

scant 1 cup confectioners' sugar

1 tsp lemon juice or lime juice

Preheat the oven to 350°F/180°C. Put 12 paper cases in a muffin pan or put 12 double-layer paper cases on a baking sheet.

Finely chop the pineapple slices. Put the butter and sugar in a bowl and beat together until light and fluffy. Gradually beat in the egg. Add the flour and, using a large metal spoon, fold into the mixture. Fold in the chopped pineapple and the pineapple juice. Spoon the batter into the paper cases.

Bake the cupcakes in the preheated oven for 20 minutes, or until well risen and golden brown. Transfer to a wire rack and let cool.

To make the frosting, put the butter and cream cheese in a large bowl and, using an electric handheld mixer, beat together until smooth. Add the rind from the lemon or lime. Sift the confectioners' sugar into the mixture, then beat together until well mixed. Gradually beat in the juice from the lemon or lime, adding enough to form a spreading consistency.

When the cupcakes are cold, spread the frosting on top of each cake, or fill a pastry bag fitted with a large star tip and pipe the frosting on top. Store the cupcakes in the refrigerator until ready to serve.

Macadamia & Maple Cupcakes

makes 10

6 tbsp butter, softened

¼ cup soft brown sugar

2 tbsp maple syrup

1 large egg, lightly beaten

⅔ cup self-rising flour

½ cup macadamia nuts, chopped

1 tbsp milk

for the frosting

2 tbsp butter, softened

2 tbsp maple syrup

¾ cup confectioners' sugar, sifted

⅓ cup cream cheese

2 tbsp chopped macadamia nuts, lightly toasted

Preheat the oven to 375°F/190°C. Put 10 paper cases in a muffin pan or put 10 double-layer paper cases on a baking sheet.

Put the butter, sugar, and maple syrup in a bowl and beat together until light and fluffy. Gradually beat in the egg. Sift in the flour and, using a metal spoon, fold into the mixture with the nuts and milk. Spoon the mixture into the paper cases.

Bake the cupcakes in the preheated oven for 20 minutes, or until golden brown and firm to the touch. Transfer to a wire rack and let cool.

To make the frosting, beat the butter and maple syrup together until smooth. Sift in the confectioners' sugar and beat in thoroughly. Gently beat in the cream cheese. Swirl the frosting on the top of each cake and sprinkle over the toasted nuts.

Cranberry Cupcakes

makes 14

5½ tbsp butter, softened

½ cup superfine sugar

1 large egg

2 tbsp milk

¾ cup self-rising flour

1 tsp baking powder

scant ¾ cup cranberries, frozen

Preheat the oven to 350°F/180°C. Put 14 paper cases in 2 muffin pans or put 14 double-layer paper cases on a baking sheet.

Put the butter and sugar in a bowl and beat together until light and fluffy. Gradually beat in the egg, then stir in the milk. Sift in the flour and baking powder and, using a large metal spoon, fold them into the mixture. Gently fold in the frozen cranberries. Spoon the batter into the paper cases.

Bake the cupcakes in the preheated oven for 15–20 minutes, or until well risen and golden brown. Transfer to a wire rack and let cool.

Pistachio Cupcakes with Tangy Lime Frosting

makes 16

generous ¾ cup unsalted pistachio nuts

½ cup butter, softened

¾ cup superfine sugar

1 cup self-rising flour

2 eggs, lightly beaten

4 tbsp strained plain yogurt

for the frosting

½ cup butter, softened

2 tbsp sweetened lime juice

few drops green food coloring (optional)

1¾ cups confectioners' sugar

1 tbsp pistachio nuts, chopped

Preheat the oven to 350°F/180°C. Put 16 paper cases in 2 muffin pans or put 16 double-layer paper cases on a baking sheet.

Put the pistachio nuts in a food processor or blender and process for a few seconds until finely ground. Add the butter, sugar, flour, eggs, and yogurt and process until evenly mixed. Spoon the mixture into the paper cases.

Bake the cupcakes in the preheated oven for 20–25 minutes, or until golden brown and firm to the touch. Transfer to a wire rack and let cool.

To make the frosting, put the butter, lime juice, and food coloring (if using) in a bowl and beat until fluffy. Sift in the confectioners' sugar and beat until smooth. Swirl the frosting over each cupcake and sprinkle with the chopped pistachio nuts.

Apple Streusel Cupcakes

makes 14

½ tsp baking soda

10-oz/280-g jar tart applesauce

4 tbsp butter, softened

generous ⅜ cup raw brown sugar

1 large egg, lightly beaten

scant 1¼ cups self-rising white flour

½ tsp ground cinnamon

½ tsp freshly ground nutmeg

for the topping

generous ⅓ cup all-purpose flour

¼ cup raw brown sugar

¼ tsp ground cinnamon

¼ tsp freshly grated nutmeg

2½ tbsp butter

Preheat the oven to 350°F/180°C. Put 14 paper cases in 2 muffin pans or put 14 double-layer paper cases on a baking sheet.

First make the topping. Put the flour, sugar, cinnamon, and nutmeg in a bowl or in the bowl of a food processor. Cut the butter into small pieces, then either rub it in by hand or blend in the processor until the mixture resembles fine bread crumbs. Set aside while you make the cakes.

To make the cupcakes, add the baking soda to the jar of applesauce and stir until dissolved. Put the butter and sugar in a bowl and beat together until light and fluffy. Gradually beat in the egg. Sift in the flour, cinnamon, and nutmeg and, using a large metal spoon, fold into the mixture, alternating with the applesauce.

Spoon the batter into the paper cases. Sprinkle the topping over each cupcake to cover the tops and press down gently.

Bake the cupcakes in the preheated oven for 20 minutes, or until well risen and golden brown. Leave the cakes for 2–3 minutes before serving warm or transfer to a wire rack and let cool.

Carrot & Orange Cupcakes with Mascarpone Frosting

makes 12

8 tbsp butter, softened

generous ½ cup firmly packed brown sugar

juice and finely grated rind of 1 small orange

2 large eggs, lightly beaten

6 oz/175 g carrots, grated

¼ cup walnut pieces, coarsely chopped

scant 1 cup all-purpose flour

1 tsp ground pumpkin pie spice

1½ tsp baking powder

for the frosting

1¼ cups mascarpone cheese

4 tbsp confectioners' sugar

grated rind of 1 large orange

Preheat the oven to 350°F/180°C. Put 12 muffin paper cases in a muffin pan or put 12 double-layer paper cases on a baking sheet.

Put the butter, sugar, and orange rind in a bowl and beat together until light and fluffy. Gradually add the eggs, beating well after each addition. Squeeze any excess liquid from the carrots and add to the mixture with the walnuts and orange juice. Stir into the mixture until well mixed. Sift the flour, pumpkin pie spice, and baking powder and then, using a metal spoon, fold into the mixture. Spoon the batter into the paper cases.

Bake the cupcakes in the preheated oven for 25 minutes, or until well risen, firm to the touch, and golden brown. Transfer to a wire rack and let cool.

To make the frosting, put the mascarpone cheese, confectioners' sugar, and orange rind in a large bowl and beat together until well mixed.

When the cupcakes are cold, spread the frosting on top of each cupcake, swirling it with a round-bladed knife. Store the cupcakes in the refrigerator until ready to serve.

Mango & Passion Fruit Cupcakes

makes 18

½ cup butter, softened

generous ½ cup superfine sugar

1 tsp finely grated orange rind

2 eggs, lightly beaten

generous ¾ cup self-rising flour

2 oz/55 g dried mango, finely chopped

1 tbsp orange juice

for the frosting

1¾ cups confectioners' sugar

seeds and pulp from 1 passion fruit

2 tbsp orange juice

Preheat the oven to 375°F/190°C. Put 18 paper cases in 2 muffin pans or put 18 double-layer paper cases on 2 baking sheets.

Put the butter, sugar, and orange rind in a mixing bowl and beat together until light and fluffy. Gradually beat in the eggs. Sift in the flour and, using a metal spoon, fold into the mixture with the chopped mango and orange juice. Spoon the mixture into the paper cases.

Bake the cupcakes in the preheated oven for 20 minutes, or until golden brown and firm to the touch. Transfer to a wire rack and let cool.

To make the frosting, sift the confectioners' sugar into a bowl and add the passion fruit seeds and pulp and 1 tbsp of the orange juice. Mix to a smooth frosting, adding the rest of the juice if necessary. Spoon the frosting over the cupcakes. Let set.

Shredded Orange Cupcakes

makes 12

6 tbsp butter, softened

generous ⅜ cup superfine sugar

1 large egg, lightly beaten

scant ⅝ cup self-rising flour

generous ¼ cup ground almonds

grated rind and juice of 1 small orange

for the topping

grated rind and juice of 1 small orange

generous ¼ cup superfine sugar

⅛ cup toasted slivered almonds

Preheat the oven to 350°F/180°C. Put 12 paper cases in a muffin pan or put 12 double-layer paper cases on a baking sheet.

Put the butter and sugar in a bowl and beat together until light and fluffy. Gradually beat in the egg. Add the flour, ground almonds, and orange rind and, using a large metal spoon, fold into the mixture. Fold in the orange juice. Spoon the batter into the paper cases.

Bake the cupcakes in the preheated oven for 20–25 minutes, or until well risen and golden brown.

Meanwhile, make the topping. Using a citrus zester, pare the rind from the orange, then squeeze the juice. Put the rind, juice, and sugar in a pan and heat gently, stirring, until the sugar has dissolved, then let simmer for 5 minutes.

When the cupcakes have cooked, prick them all over with a skewer. Spoon the warm syrup and rind over each cupcake, then sprinkle the slivered almonds on top. Transfer to a wire rack and let cool.

Toffee Apple Cupcakes

makes 18

2 apples

1 tbsp lemon juice

2¼ cups all-purpose flour

2 tsp baking powder

1½ tsp ground cinnamon

heaping ¼ cup light brown sugar

4 tbsp butter, plus extra for greasing

scant ½ cup milk

scant ½ cup apple juice

1 egg, beaten

for the topping

2 tbsp light cream

3 tbsp light brown sugar

1 tbsp butter

Preheat the oven to 400°F/200°C. Grease two 9-cup muffin pans, preferably nonstick.

Core and coarsely grate one of the apples. Slice the remaining apple into ¼ inch/5 mm thick wedges and toss in the lemon juice. Sift together the flour, baking powder, and cinnamon, then stir in the sugar and grated apple.

Melt the butter and mix with the milk, apple juice, and egg. Stir the liquid mixture into the dry ingredients, mixing lightly until just combined. Spoon the mixture into the prepared muffin pan. Put two apple slices on top of each cake.

Bake in the preheated oven for 20–25 minutes, or until risen, firm, and golden brown. Run a knife around the edge of each cake to loosen, then turn out onto a wire rack to cool.

For the topping, place all the ingredients in a small pan and heat, stirring, until the sugar has dissolved. Increase the heat and boil rapidly for 2 minutes, or until slightly thickened and syrupy. Cool slightly, then drizzle over the cakes and let set.

Raspberry Almond Cupcakes

makes 14

½ cup butter, softened

scant ½ cup superfine sugar

½ tsp almond extract

2 eggs, lightly beaten

scant ⅔ cup self-rising flour

scant ⅔ cup ground almonds

3 oz/85 g fresh raspberries

2 tbsp slivered almonds

confectioners' sugar, for dusting

Preheat the oven to 350°F/180°C. Put 14 paper cases in 2 muffin pans or put 14 double-layer paper cases on a baking sheet.

Put the butter, sugar, and almond extract in a bowl and beat together until light and fluffy. Gradually beat in the eggs. Sift in the flour and, using a metal spoon, fold into the mixture with the ground almonds. Gently fold in the raspberries. Spoon the mixture into the paper cases. Scatter the slivered almonds over the top.

Bake the cupcakes in the preheated oven for 25–30 minutes, or until golden brown and firm to the touch. Transfer to a wire rack and let cool. Dust with confectioners' sugar.

Coconut Cherry Cupcakes

makes 12

8 tbsp butter, softened

generous ½ cup superfine sugar

2 tbsp milk

2 eggs, lightly beaten

scant ⅝ cup self-rising flour

½ tsp baking powder

⅔ cup dry unsweetened coconut

4 oz/115 g candied cherries, quartered

12 whole candied, maraschino, or fresh cherries, to decorate

for the frosting

4 tbsp butter, softened

1 cup confectioners' sugar

1 tbsp milk

Preheat the oven to 350°F/180°C. Put 12 paper cases in a muffin pan or put 12 double-layer paper cases on a baking sheet.

Put the butter and sugar in a bowl and beat together until light and fluffy. Stir in the milk. Gradually add the eggs, beating well after each addition. Sift in the flour and baking powder and fold them in with the coconut. Gently fold in most of the quartered cherries. Spoon the batter into the paper cases and sprinkle the remaining quartered cherries on top.

Bake the cupcakes in the preheated oven for 20–25 minutes, or until well risen, golden brown, and firm to the touch. Transfer to a wire rack and let cool.

To make the frosting, put the butter in a bowl and beat until fluffy. Sift in the confectioners' sugar and beat together until well mixed, gradually beating in the milk.

To decorate the cupcakes, using a pastry bag fitted with a large star tip, pipe the buttercream on top of each cupcake, then add a candied, maraschino, or fresh cherry to decorate.

Banana & Pecan Cupcakes

makes 24

scant 1⅝ cups all-purpose flour

1¼ tsp baking powder

¼ tsp baking soda

2 ripe bananas

8 tbsp butter, softened

generous ½ cup superfine sugar

½ tsp vanilla extract

2 eggs, lightly beaten

4 tbsp sour cream

½ cup pecans, coarsely chopped

for the topping

8 tbsp butter, softened

1 cup confectioners' sugar

¼ cup pecans, chopped

Preheat the oven to 375°F/190°C. Put 24 paper cases in 2 muffin pans or put 24 double-layer paper cases on 2 baking sheets.

Sift together the flour, baking powder, and baking soda. Peel the bananas, put them in a bowl, and mash with a fork.

Put the butter, sugar, and vanilla in a bowl and beat together until light and fluffy. Gradually add the eggs, beating well after each addition. Stir in the mashed bananas and sour cream. Using a metal spoon, fold in the sifted flour mixture and chopped nuts, then spoon the batter into the paper cases.

Bake the cupcakes in the preheated oven for 20 minutes, or until well risen and golden brown. Transfer to a wire rack and let cool.

To make the topping, put the butter in a bowl and beat until fluffy. Sift in the confectioners' sugar and mix together well. Spread the frosting on top of each cupcake and sprinkle with the chopped pecans before serving.

Lemon Crunch Cupcakes

makes 12

¾ cup butter, softened

generous ¾ cup superfine sugar

1¼ cups self-rising flour

1 tsp baking powder

3 large eggs

3 tbsp lemon curd

for the topping

½ cup granulated sugar

juice and grated rind 1 lemon

Preheat the oven to 350°F/180°C. Put 12 paper cases in a muffin pan or put 12 double-layer paper cases on a baking sheet.

Put the butter, sugar, flour, baking powder, and eggs in a large bowl and, using an electric handheld mixer, beat until the mixture is thoroughly blended. Fold in the lemon curd. Spoon the mixture into the paper cases.

Bake the cupcakes in the preheated oven for 20 minutes, or until risen and golden brown. While the cupcakes are baking, mix the topping ingredients together in a bowl.

Remove the cupcakes from the oven and let stand for 2 minutes, then spread some of the topping over each cupcake. Let cool in the pan—the topping will turn crisp on cooling.

Moist Walnut Cupcakes

makes 12

¾ cup walnuts

4 tbsp butter, softened

½ cup superfine sugar

grated rind of ½ lemon

½ cup self-rising flour

2 eggs

12 walnut halves,
to decorate

for the frosting

4 tbsp butter, softened

¾ cup confectioners' sugar

grated rind of ½ lemon

1 tsp lemon juice

Preheat the oven to 375°F/190°C. Put 12 paper cases in a muffin pan or put 12 double-layer paper cases on a baking sheet.

Put the walnuts in a food processor and, using a pulsating action, blend until finely ground, being careful not to overgrind, which will turn them to oil. Add the butter, cut into small pieces, along with the sugar, lemon rind, flour, and eggs, then blend until evenly mixed. Spoon the batter into the paper cases.

Bake the cupcakes in the preheated oven for 20 minutes, or until well risen and golden brown. Transfer to a wire rack and let cool.

To make the frosting, put the butter in a bowl and beat until fluffy. Sift in the confectioners' sugar, add the lemon rind and juice, and mix well together.

When the cupcakes are cold, spread the frosting on top of each cupcake and top with a walnut half to decorate.

4

Something
Special

Black Forest Cupcakes

makes 12

3 oz/75 g dark chocolate

1 tsp lemon juice

4 tbsp milk

generous 1 cup self-rising flour

1 tbsp cocoa powder

½ tsp baking soda

2 eggs

4 tbsp butter, softened

generous ½ cup light brown sugar

1 oz/25 g dried and sweetened sour cherries, chopped

2 tbsp cherry liqueur (optional)

⅔ cup heavy cream, softly whipped

5 tbsp cherry conserve

cocoa powder, to dust

Preheat the oven to 350°F/180°C. Put 12 paper cases in a muffin pan or put 12 double-layer paper cases on a baking sheet.

Break the chocolate into a heatproof bowl and set the bowl over a saucepan of gently simmering water until melted. Add the lemon juice to the milk and let stand for 10 minutes—the milk will curdle a little.

Sift the flour, cocoa powder, and baking soda into a bowl. Add the eggs, butter, sugar, and milk mixture and beat with an electric handheld mixer until smooth. Fold in the melted chocolate and cherries. Spoon the mixture into the paper cases.

Bake the cupcakes in the preheated oven for 20–25 minutes, until risen and firm to the touch. Transfer to a wire rack and let cool.

When the cupcakes are cold, use a serrated knife to cut a circle from the top of each cupcake. Sprinkle the cakes with a little cherry liqueur, if using. Spoon the whipped cream into the centers and top with a small spoonful of conserve. Gently replace the cupcake tops and dust lightly with cocoa powder. Store in the refrigerator until ready to serve.

Birthday Party Cupcakes

makes 24

1 cup soft margarine

generous 1⅛ cups superfine sugar

4 eggs

scant 1⅝ cups self-rising flour

for the topping

¾ cup butter, softened

3 cups confectioners' sugar

a variety of small candies and chocolates, sugar-coated chocolates, dried fruits, edible sugar flower shapes, cake decorating sprinkles, silver dragées (cake decoration balls), and sugar strands

various colored tubes of writing frosting

24 birthday cake candles (optional)

Preheat the oven to 350°F/180°C. Put 24 paper cases in 2 muffin pans or put 24 double-layer paper cases on 2 baking sheets.

Put the margarine, sugar, eggs, and flour in a large bowl and, using an electric handheld mixer, beat together until just smooth. Spoon the batter into the paper cases.

Bake the cupcakes in the preheated oven for 15–20 minutes, or until well risen, golden brown, and firm to the touch. Transfer to a wire rack and let cool.

To make the topping, put the butter in a bowl and beat until fluffy. Sift in the confectioners' sugar and beat together until smooth and creamy.

When the cupcakes are cold, spread the frosting on top of each cupcake, then decorate to your choice and, if desired, place a candle in the top of each.

Halloween Cupcakes

makes 12

8 tbsp soft margarine

generous ½ cup superfine sugar

2 eggs

generous ¾ cup self-rising flour

for the topping

7 oz/200 g orange ready-to-roll colored fondant frosting

confectioners' sugar, for dusting

2 oz/55 g black ready-to-roll colored fondant frosting

black cake-writing frosting

yellow cake-writing frosting

Preheat the oven to 350°F/180°C. Put 12 paper cases in a muffin pan or put 12 double-layer paper cases on a baking sheet.

Put the margarine, sugar, eggs, and flour in a bowl and, using an electric handheld mixer, beat together until smooth. Spoon the batter into the cases.

Bake the cupcakes in the preheated oven for 15–20 minutes, or until well risen, golden brown, and firm to the touch. Transfer to a wire rack and let cool.

When the cupcakes are cold, knead the orange frosting until pliable, then roll out on a counter dusted with confectioners' sugar. Using the palm of your hand, lightly rub confectioners' sugar into the frosting to prevent it from spotting. Using a 2¼-inch/5.5-cm plain round cutter, cut out 12 circles, rerolling the frosting as necessary. Place a circle on top of each cupcake.

Roll out the black frosting on a counter lightly dusted with confectioners' sugar. Using the palm of your hand, lightly rub confectioners' sugar into the frosting to prevent it from spotting. Using a 1¼-inch/3-cm plain round cutter, cut out 12 circles and place them on the center of the cupcakes. Using black writing frosting, pipe 8 legs onto each spider and using yellow writing frosting, draw 2 eyes and a mouth.

Valentine Heart Cupcakes

makes 6

6 tbsp butter, softened

generous ⅜ cup superfine sugar

½ tsp vanilla extract

2 eggs, lightly beaten

½ cup all-purpose flour

1 tbsp unsweetened cocoa

1 tsp baking powder

for the marzipan hearts

1¼ oz/35 g marzipan

red food coloring (liquid or paste)

confectioners' sugar, for dusting

for the topping

4 tbsp butter, softened

1 cup confectioners' sugar

1 oz/25 g semisweet chocolate, melted

6 chocolate flowers, to decorate

To make the hearts, knead the marzipan until pliable, then add a few drops of red coloring and knead until evenly colored red. Roll out the marzipan to a thickness of ¼ inch/5 mm on a counter dusted with confectioners' sugar. Using a small heart-shaped cutter, cut out 6 hearts. Put these on a tray lined with waxed paper and dusted with confectioners' sugar. Let dry for 3–4 hours.

To make the cupcakes, preheat the oven to 350°F/180°C. Put 6 muffin paper cases in a muffin pan or put 6 double-layer paper cases on a baking sheet.

Put the butter, sugar, and vanilla extract in a bowl and beat together until light and fluffy. Gradually add the eggs, beating well after each addition. Sift in the flour, cocoa, and baking powder and, using a large metal spoon, fold into the mixture. Spoon the batter into the paper cases.

Bake the cupcakes in the preheated oven for 20–25 minutes, or until well risen and firm to the touch. Transfer to a wire rack and let cool.

To make the topping, put the butter in a large bowl and beat until fluffy. Sift in the confectioners' sugar and beat together until smooth. Add the melted chocolate and beat together until well mixed. When the cakes are cold, spread the topping on top of each cake, decorate with the chocolate flowers, and add the marzipan hearts.

Strawberry & Cream Cupcakes

makes 10

6 tbsp unsalted butter, softened

scant ½ cup superfine sugar

½ tsp vanilla extract

1 large egg, lightly beaten

scant ⅔ cup self-rising flour

1 tbsp milk

¼ cup raisins

4 oz/115 g small strawberries, hulled and sliced

1 tbsp strawberry conserve

½ cup heavy cream, whipped

confectioners' sugar, for dusting

Preheat the oven to 375°F/190°C. Put 10 paper cases in a muffin pan or put 10 double-layer paper cases on a baking sheet.

Put the butter, sugar, and vanilla extract in a mixing bowl and beat together until light and fluffy. Gradually beat in the egg. Sift in the flour and, using a metal spoon, fold into the mixture with the milk and raisins. Spoon the mixture into the paper cases.

Bake the cupcakes in the preheated oven for 15–20 minutes, or until golden brown and firm to the touch. Transfer to a wire rack and let cool.

When the cupcakes are cold, use a serrated knife to cut a circle from the top of each cupcake. Gently mix the strawberries and conserve together and divide between the cupcakes. Top each with a small dollop of the whipped cream. Replace the cake tops and dust with confectioners' sugar. Store the cupcakes in the refrigerator until ready to serve.

Feather-Iced Coffee Cupcakes

makes 18

1 tbsp instant coffee granules

1 tbsp boiling water

8 tbsp butter, softened

generous ½ cup firmly packed brown sugar

2 eggs

generous ¾ cup self-rising flour

½ tsp baking powder

2 tbsp sour cream

for the frosting

2 cups confectioners' sugar

4 tsp warm water

1 tsp instant coffee granules

2 tsp boiling water

Preheat the oven to 375°F/190°C. Put 18 paper cases in 2 muffin pans or put 18 double-layer paper cases on 2 baking sheets.

Put the coffee granules in a cup or small bowl, add the boiling water, and stir until dissolved. Let cool slightly.

Put the butter, sugar, and eggs in a bowl. Sift in the flour and baking powder, then beat the ingredients together until smooth. Add the dissolved coffee and the sour cream and beat together until well mixed. Spoon the batter into the paper cases.

Bake the cupcakes in the preheated oven for 20 minutes, or until well risen and golden brown. Transfer to a wire rack and let cool.

To make the frosting, sift ¾ cup of the confectioners' sugar into a bowl, then gradually mix in the warm water to make a coating consistency that will cover the back of a wooden spoon. Dissolve the coffee granules in the boiling water. Sift the remaining confectioners' sugar into a bowl, then stir in the dissolved coffee granules. Spoon the frosting into a pastry bag fitted with a piping tip. When the cupcakes are cold, coat the tops with the white frosting, then quickly pipe the coffee frosting in parallel lines on top. Using a skewer, draw it across the piped lines in both directions. Let set before serving.

Marzipan Flower Cupcakes

makes 12

generous ¾ cup self-rising flour

½ tsp baking powder

½ cup soft margarine

generous ½ cup superfine sugar

2 eggs, lightly beaten

few drops almond extract

for the topping

7 oz/200 g natural marzipan

confectioners' sugar, for dusting

2 tbsp apricot jam

Preheat the oven to 350°F/180°C. Put 12 paper cases in a muffin pan or put 12 double-layer paper cases on a baking sheet.

Sift the flour and baking powder into a bowl. Add the margarine, sugar, eggs, and almond extract and, using an electric handheld mixer, beat together until smooth. Spoon the mixture into the paper cases.

Bake the cupcakes in the preheated oven for 20 minutes, or until golden brown and firm to the touch. Transfer to a wire rack and let cool.

For the topping, roll out the marzipan on a surface dusted lightly with confectioners' sugar. Using a 1¼-inch/3-cm round cutter, stamp out 60 circles, reusing the marzipan as necessary. Spread a little apricot jam over the top of each cupcake. Pinch the marzipan circles on one side to create petal shapes and arrange five petals on top of each cupcake. Roll small balls of remaining marzipan for the flower centers and place in the middle of the cupcakes.

Honey & Spice Cupcakes

makes 12

⅔ cup butter

scant ½ cup light brown sugar

scant ½ cup honey

1¾ cups self-rising flour

1 tsp ground allspice

2 eggs, beaten

22–24 whole blanched almonds

Preheat the oven to 350°F/180°C. Put 12 paper cases in a muffin pan or put 12 double-layer paper cases on a baking sheet.

Place the butter, sugar, and honey in a large pan and heat gently, stirring, until the butter has melted. Remove the pan from the heat.

Sift together the flour and allspice and stir into the mixture in the pan, then beat in the eggs, mixing to a smooth batter.

Spoon the batter into the paper liners and place a blanched almond on top of each one. Bake in the preheated oven for 20–25 minutes, or until well-risen and golden brown. Transfer to a wire rack to cool.

Festive Cupcakes

makes 14

4 oz/115 g mixed dried fruit

1 tsp finely grated orange rind

2 tbsp brandy or orange juice

6 tbsp butter, softened

scant ½ cup soft brown sugar

1 large egg, lightly beaten

generous ¾ cup self-rising flour

1 tsp ground allspice

1 tbsp silver dragées (cake decoration balls), to decorate

for the frosting

¾ cup confectioners' sugar

2 tbsp orange juice

Put the mixed fruit, orange rind, and brandy or orange juice in a small bowl, cover, and let soak for 1 hour.

Preheat the oven to 375°F/190°C. Put 14 paper cases in 2 muffin pans or put 14 double-layer paper cases on a baking sheet.

Put the butter and sugar in a mixing bowl and beat together until light and fluffy. Gradually beat in the egg. Sift in the flour and allspice and, using a metal spoon, fold them into the mixture followed by the soaked fruit. Spoon the mixture into the paper cases.

Bake the cupcakes in the preheated oven for 15–20 minutes, or until golden brown and firm to the touch. Transfer to a wire rack and let cool.

To make the frosting, sift the confectioners' sugar into a bowl and gradually mix in enough orange juice until the mixture is smooth and thick enough to coat the back of a wooden spoon. Using a teaspoon, drizzle the frosting in a zigzag pattern over the cupcakes. Decorate with the silver dragées. Let set.

Gold & Silver Anniversary Cupcakes

makes 24

1 cup butter, softened

generous 1 cup superfine sugar

1 tsp vanilla extract

4 large eggs, lightly beaten

scant 1⅝ cups self-rising flour

5 tbsp milk

for the topping

¾ cup unsalted butter

3 cups confectioners' sugar

silver or gold dragées (cake decoration balls)

Preheat the oven to 350°F/180°C. Put 24 silver or gold foil cake cases in muffin pans, or arrange them on baking sheets.

Put the butter, sugar, and vanilla extract in a bowl and beat together until light and fluffy. Gradually add the eggs, beating well after each addition. Add the flour and, using a large metal spoon, fold into the mixture with the milk. Spoon the batter into the paper cases.

Bake the cupcakes in the preheated oven for 15–20 minutes, or until well risen and firm to the touch. Transfer to a wire rack and let cool.

To make the topping, put the butter in a large bowl and beat until fluffy. Sift in the confectioners' sugar and beat together until well mixed. Put the topping in a pastry bag, fitted with a medium star-shaped tip.

When the cupcakes are cold, pipe frosting over the top of each one. Sprinkle over the silver or gold dragées before serving.

Gold Star Cupcakes

makes 12

6 tbsp butter, softened

scant ½ cup light brown sugar

1 large egg, beaten

scant ⅔ cup self-rising flour

½ tsp ground cinnamon

1 tbsp milk

for the gold stars

3 oz/ 85 g yellow ready-to-roll colored fondant

confectioners' sugar, for dusting

edible gold dusting powder (optional)

for the frosting

¾ cup confectioners' sugar

2–3 tsp lemon juice

Preheat the oven to 350°F/180°C. Put 12 paper cases in a muffin pan or put 12 double-layer paper cases on a baking sheet.

Put the butter and sugar in a mixing bowl and beat together until light and fluffy. Gradually beat in the egg. Sift in the flour and cinnamon and, using a metal spoon, fold them into the mixture with the milk. Spoon the mixture into the paper cases.

Bake the cupcakes in the preheated oven for 20 minutes, or until golden brown and firm to the touch. Transfer to a wire rack and let cool.

To make the gold stars, roll the yellow fondant out on a surface lightly dusted with confectioners' sugar and, using a small star cutter, stamp out 12 stars. Brush each star with a little gold dusting powder, if using. Set aside on a sheet of parchment paper.

To make the frosting, sift the confectioners' sugar into a bowl and stir in enough lemon juice to make a smooth and thick frosting.

Spoon the frosting on top of the cupcakes and top each with a gold star. Let set.

Baby Shower Cupcakes with Sugared Almonds

makes 24

1¾ cups butter, softened

2 cups superfine sugar

finely grated rind of
2 lemons

8 eggs, lightly beaten

generous 2¾ cups
self-rising flour

for the topping

3 cups confectioners' sugar

red or blue food coloring
(liquid or paste)

24 sugared almonds

Preheat the oven to 350°F/180°C. Put 24 paper cases in
2 muffin pans or put 24 double-layer paper cases on a large
baking sheet.

Put the butter, sugar, and lemon rind in a bowl and beat
together until light and fluffy. Gradually add the eggs, beating
well after each addition. Add the flour and, using a large metal
spoon, fold into the mixture. Spoon the batter into the paper
cases to half-fill them.

Bake the cupcakes in the preheated oven for 20–25 minutes,
or until well risen, golden brown, and firm to the touch. Transfer
to a wire rack and let cool.

When the cakes are cold, make the topping. Sift the
confectioners' sugar into a bowl. Add 6–8 teaspoons of hot
water and stir until the mixture is smooth and thick enough to
coat the back of a wooden spoon. Dip a skewer into the red or
blue food coloring, then stir it into the frosting until it is evenly
colored pink or pale blue.

Spoon the frosting on top of each cupcake. Top each with a
sugared almond and let set for about 30 minutes before serving.

Easter Cupcakes

makes 12

8 tbsp butter, softened

generous ½ cup superfine sugar

2 eggs, lightly beaten

scant ⅝ cup self-rising flour

generous ¼ cup unsweetened cocoa

for the topping

6 tbsp butter, softened

1½ cups confectioners' sugar

1 tbsp milk

2–3 drops of vanilla extract

two 4¾-oz/130-g packages mini chocolate candy shell eggs

Preheat the oven to 350°F/180°C. Put 12 paper cases in a muffin pan or put 12 double-layer paper cases on a baking sheet.

Put the butter and sugar in a bowl and beat together until light and fluffy. Gradually add the eggs, beating well after each addition. Sift in the flour and cocoa and, using a large metal spoon, fold into the mixture. Spoon the batter into the paper cases.

Bake the cupcakes in the preheated oven for 15–20 minutes, or until well risen and firm to the touch. Transfer to a wire rack and let cool.

To make the topping, put the butter in a bowl and beat until fluffy. Sift in the confectioners' sugar and beat together until well mixed, adding the milk and vanilla extract.

When the cupcakes are cold, put the frosting in a pastry bag, fitted with a large star tip, and pipe a circle around the edge of each cupcake to form a nest. Place chocolate eggs in the center of each nest, to decorate.

Christmas Cupcakes

makes 18

9 tbsp butter, softened

1 cup superfine sugar

4–6 drops almond extract

4 eggs, lightly beaten

generous 1 cup self-rising flour

1¾ cups ground almonds

for the topping

1 lb/450 g white ready-to-roll fondant frosting

2 oz/55 g green ready-to-roll colored fondant frosting

1 oz/25 g red ready-to-roll colored fondant frosting

confectioners' sugar, for dusting

Preheat the oven to 350°F/180°C. Put 18 paper cases in 2 muffin pans or put 18 double-layer paper cases on a large baking sheet.

Put the butter, sugar, and almond extract in a bowl and beat together until light and fluffy. Gradually add the eggs, beating well after each addition. Add the flour and, using a large metal spoon, fold it into the mixture, then fold in the ground almonds. Spoon the batter into the paper cases to half-fill them.

Bake the cakes in the preheated oven for 20 minutes, or until well risen, golden brown, and firm to the touch. Transfer to a wire rack and let cool.

When the cakes are cold, knead the white frosting until pliable, then roll out on a counter lightly dusted with confectioners' sugar. Using a 2¾-inch/7-cm plain round cutter, cut out 16 circles, rerolling the frosting as necessary. Place a circle on top of each cupcake.

Roll out the green frosting on a counter lightly dusted with confectioners' sugar. Using the palm of your hand, rub confectioners' sugar into the frosting to prevent it from spotting. Using a holly leaf-shaped cutter, cut out 32 leaves, rerolling the frosting as necessary. Brush each leaf with a little cooled boiled water and place 2 leaves on top of each cake. Roll the red frosting between the palms of your hands to form 48 berries and place in the center of the leaves.

Vanilla Frosted Cupcakes

makes 12

4 oz/115 g butter, softened

4 oz/115 g superfine sugar

2 eggs, lightly beaten

4 oz/115 g self-rising flour

1 tbsp milk

1 tbsp hundreds and thousands

for the frosting

6 oz/175 g unsalted butter, softened

1 tsp vanilla extract

10 oz/280 g confectioners' sugar

Preheat the oven to 350°F/180°C. Put 12 paper cases in a muffin pan or put 12 double-layer paper cases on a baking sheet.

Put the butter and sugar in a bowl and beat together until light and fluffy. Gradually beat in the eggs. Sift over the flour and, using a metal spoon, fold into the mixture with the milk. Spoon the mixture into the paper cases.

Bake the cupcakes in the preheated oven for 20 minutes or until golden brown and firm to the touch. Transfer to a wire rack and leave to cool.

To make the frosting, put the butter and vanilla extract in a bowl and, using an electric handheld whisk, beat until the butter is pale and very soft. Gradually sift in the confectioners' sugar, whisking well after each addition. Spoon the frosting into a large piping bag fitted with a medium star-shaped nozzle and pipe large swirls of frosting on the top of each cupcake. Sprinkle with hundreds and thousands.

5

Cake in a
Cup

Cherry Almond Cupcakes

makes 4

4 tbsp butter, softened, plus extra for greasing

¼ cup superfine sugar

1 large egg, lightly beaten

generous ⅓ cup self-rising flour

scant ½ cup ground almonds

½ tsp almond extract

1 tbsp milk

¼ cup candied cherries, quartered

1 tbsp toasted slivered almonds, to decorate

for the frosting

⅓ cup confectioners' sugar

2 tsp lemon juice

Preheat the oven to 350°F/180°C. Grease four 1-cup ovenproof dishes (such as ramekins) with butter.

Put the butter and sugar in a bowl and beat together until light and fluffy. Gradually beat in the egg. Sift in the flour and, using a metal spoon, fold into the mixture with the ground almonds, almond extract, and milk. Spoon the mixture into the dishes. Scatter over the cherries.

Put the dishes on a baking sheet and bake in the preheated oven for 25–30 minutes, or until risen, golden brown, and firm to the touch. Let cool.

To make the frosting, sift the confectioners' sugar into a bowl and stir in the lemon juice to make a smooth frosting. Using a teaspoon, drizzle the frosting over the cupcakes and decorate with slivered almonds. Let set.

Hot Pecan Brownie Cupcakes

makes 6

½ cup butter, plus extra for greasing

4 oz/115 g dark chocolate, broken into pieces

2 eggs

generous ½ cup light brown sugar

3 tbsp maple syrup

generous ¾ cup all-purpose flour, sifted

½ cup pecan nuts, chopped

crème fraîche or heavy cream, to serve

Preheat the oven to 350°F/180°C. Grease six ¾-cup ovenproof dishes (such as ramekins) with butter.

Put the chocolate and butter into a heatproof bowl set over a saucepan of gently simmering water until melted, stirring occasionally. Cool for 5 minutes.

Put the eggs, sugar, and maple syrup in a bowl and whisk together until well blended. Whisk in the chocolate mixture, then fold in the flour and two-thirds of the pecan nuts. Pour the mixture into the dishes and scatter over the rest of the nuts.

Put the dishes on a baking sheet and bake in the preheated oven for 25–30 minutes, or until the cupcakes have risen and are crisp on top but still feel slightly wobbly if lightly pressed. Serve hot topped with a spoonful of crème fraîche or heavy cream.

Blackberry Crumble Cupcakes

makes 6

½ cup butter, softened, plus extra for greasing

generous ¾ cup self-rising flour

½ tsp baking powder

generous ½ cup superfine sugar

2 eggs

6 oz/175 g blackberries

whipped cream, to serve

for the topping

scant ⅔ cup self-rising flour

¼ cup raw brown sugar

4 tbsp butter, chilled and diced

Preheat the oven to 375°F/190°C. Grease six 1-cup ovenproof dishes (such as ramekins) with butter.

To make the topping, mix the flour and sugar in a bowl. Add the butter and rub in until the mixture resembles course bread crumbs.

To make the cake, sift the flour and baking powder into a bowl. Add the butter, superfine sugar, and eggs and, using an electric handheld mixer, beat together until smooth. Spoon the mixture into the dishes and level the surface. Top with the blackberries. Spoon the crumble mixture over the blackberries.

Put the dishes on a baking sheet and bake in the preheated oven for 25–30 minutes, until the crumble topping is golden brown. Serve warm with whipped cream.

Blueberry & Buttermilk Cupcakes

makes 6

scant ⅔ cup butter, softened, plus extra for greasing

¾ cup superfine sugar

2 eggs, lightly beaten

4 tbsp cultured buttermilk

1¼ cups self-rising flour

4 oz/115 g blueberries

confectioners' sugar, for dusting

Preheat the oven to 375°F/190°C. Grease six 1-cup ovenproof dishes (such as ramekins) with butter.

Put the butter and sugar in a bowl and beat together until light and fluffy. Gradually beat in the eggs. Stir in the buttermilk. Sift in the flour and, using a metal spoon, fold into the mixture. Gently fold in half the blueberries. Spoon the mixture into the dishes. Scatter over the rest of the blueberries.

Put the dishes on a baking sheet and bake in the preheated oven for 25 minutes, until the cakes have risen and are firm to the touch. Serve warm or cold, dusted with sifted confectioners' sugar.

Hot Marmalade Cupcakes

makes 4

1 small orange

6 tbsp butter, softened, plus extra for greasing

scant ½ cup superfine sugar

1 large egg, lightly beaten

generous ¾ cup self-rising flour

2 tbsp fine shred marmalade, warmed

crème fraîche or heavy cream, to serve

Put the orange in a saucepan and cover with water. Bring to a boil, then reduce the heat, cover, and simmer for 1 hour, until soft. Remove the orange from the water and let cool for 30 minutes.

Preheat the oven to 350°F/180°C. Grease four ¾-cup ovenproof dishes (such as ramekins) with butter.

Cut the orange into chunks and remove any seeds. Put all the orange chunks (rind included) into a food processor and blend until finely minced. Add the butter, sugar, egg, and flour and process until well blended. Spoon the mixture into the dishes.

Put the dishes on a baking sheet and bake in the preheated oven for 25–30 minutes, or until risen, golden brown, and firm to the touch. Cool for 2–3 minutes, then brush the warmed marmalade over the top of each cupcake. Serve with crème fraîche or heavy cream.

Spiced Plum Cupcakes

makes 4

2 oz/55 g butter, softened, plus extra for greasing

2 oz/55 g superfine sugar

1 large egg, lightly beaten

2 oz/55 g plain whole wheat flour

½ tsp baking powder

1 tsp ground mixed spice

1 oz/25 g blanched hazelnuts, coarsely ground

2 small plums, halved, stoned and sliced

Greek-style yogurt, to serve

Preheat the oven to 350°F/180°C. Grease four 5-fl oz/150-ml ovenproof dishes (such as ramekins) with butter.

Put the butter and sugar in a bowl and beat together until light and fluffy. Gradually beat in the egg. Sift in the flour, baking powder, and mixed spice (tipping any bran left in the sieve into the bowl) and, using a metal spoon, fold into the mixture with the ground hazelnuts. Spoon the mixture into the teacups or dishes. Arrange the sliced plums on top of the mixture.

Put the cups or dishes on a baking sheet and bake in the preheated oven for 25 minutes or until risen and firm to the touch. Serve warm or cold with Greek-style yogurt.

Sticky Date & Toffee Cupcakes

makes 6

½ cup dried, pitted dates, chopped

½ tsp baking soda

⅓ cup water

6 tbsp butter, softened, plus extra for greasing

scant ½ cup dark brown sugar

1 tsp vanilla extract

2 eggs, lightly beaten

generous ½ cup self-rising flour

whipped cream, to serve

for the toffee sauce

scant ½ cup dark brown sugar

4 tbsp butter

4 tbsp double cream

Put the dates, baking soda, and water in a small saucepan and bring to a boil. Remove from the heat and set aside to cool.

Preheat the oven to 350°F/180°C. Grease six ¾-cup ovenproof dishes (such as ramekins) with butter.

Put the butter, sugar, and vanilla extract in a bowl and beat together until light and fluffy. Gradually beat in the eggs. Sift in the flour and, using a metal spoon, fold into the mixture followed by the date mixture. Spoon the mixture into the dishes.

Put the dishes on a baking sheet and bake in the preheated oven for 20–25 minutes, or until risen and firm to the touch.

To make the toffee sauce, put all the ingredients in a small saucepan and heat until the butter has melted. Simmer for 5 minutes, stirring occasionally. Using a skewer, prick a few holes in each warm cupcake and drizzle over some of the sauce. Serve the cupcakes with the rest of the toffee sauce and whipped cream.

Lemon Meringue Cupcakes

makes 4

6 tbsp butter, softened plus extra for greasing

scant ½ cup superfine sugar

finely grated rind and juice of ½ lemon

1 large egg, lightly beaten

scant ⅔ cup self-raising flour

2 tbsp lemon curd

for the meringue

2 egg whites

generous ½ cup superfine sugar

Preheat the oven to 375°F/190°C. Grease four 1-cup ovenproof dishes (such as ramekins) with butter.

Put the butter, sugar, and lemon rind in a bowl and beat together until light and fluffy. Gradually beat in the egg. Sift in the flour and, using a metal spoon, fold into the mixture with the lemon juice. Spoon the mixture into the dishes.

Put the dishes on a baking sheet and bake in the preheated oven for 15 minutes, or until risen and pale golden brown.

Whilst the cupcakes are baking, make the meringue. Put the egg whites in a clean grease-free bowl and, using a handheld electric mixer, mix until stiff. Gradually whisk in the superfine sugar to form a stiff and glossy meringue.

Spread the lemon curd over the hot cupcakes, then swirl over the meringue. Return the cupcakes to the oven for 4–5 minutes, until the meringue is golden. Serve immediately.

Banana & Toffee Cupcakes

makes 4

5 tbsp butter, softened, plus extra for greasing

½ cup light brown sugar

2 eggs, lightly beaten

¾ cup self-rising flour

1 small ripe banana, peeled and mashed

for the topping

⅔ cup heavy cream

½ banana, peeled and sliced

2 tbsp dulce de leche (toffee sauce)

1 tbsp grated chocolate

Preheat the oven to 375°F/190°C. Grease four 1-cup ovenproof dishes (such as ramekins) with butter.

Put the butter and sugar in a bowl and beat together until light and fluffy. Gradually beat in the eggs. Sift in the flour and, using a metal spoon, fold into the mixture with the mashed banana. Spoon the mixture into the dishes.

Put the dishes on a baking sheet and bake in the preheated oven for 20–25 minutes, or until risen and golden brown. Let cool.

For the topping, whisk the cream in a bowl until softly peaking. Spoon the whipped cream on top of each cupcake, then arrange 3–4 banana slices on top. Drizzle over the dulce de leche and sprinkle over the grated chocolate. Store the cupcakes in the refrigerator until ready to serve.

Warm Strawberry Cupcakes

makes 6

8 tbsp butter, softened, plus extra for greasing

4 tbsp strawberry conserve

generous ½ cup superfine sugar

2 eggs, lightly beaten

1 tsp vanilla extract

generous ¾ cup self-rising flour

1 lb/450 g small whole fresh strawberries

confectioners' sugar, for dusting

Preheat the oven to 350°F/180°C. Grease six ¾-cup ovenproof dishes (such as ramekins) with butter. Spoon 2 teaspoons of the strawberry conserve in the bottom of each dish.

Put the butter and sugar in a bowl and beat together until light and fluffy. Gradually add the eggs, beating well after each addition, then add the vanilla extract. Sift in the flour and, using a large metal spoon, fold it into the mixture. Spoon the batter into the teacups.

Stand the cups in a roasting pan, then pour in enough hot water to come one-third up the sides of the cups. Bake the cupcakes in the preheated oven for 40 minutes, or until well risen and golden brown, and a skewer, inserted in the center, comes out clean. If over-browning, cover the cupcakes with a sheet of foil. Leave the cupcakes to cool for 2–3 minutes, then carefully lift the cups from the pan and place them on saucers.

Place a few of the whole strawberries on each cake, then dust them with sifted confectioners' sugar. Serve warm with the remaining strawberries.